Nonfiction Reading and Writing Workshops

Asking Questions

Writing Focus

Compare-Contrast Essay

Text Structure

Compare-Contrast Article

Program Consultants

Stephanie Harvey
Dr. P. David Pearson

Picture Credits

Cover Keren Su/Getty Images, (objects) Steven Curtis Design; page 4 Jeff Shelly; page 5 Courtesy, Ming L. Pei, webmaster-editor, Peter Poulides/Stone, (top) illustration from *If the World Were a Village*, written by David J. Smith and illustrated by Slelagh Armstrong, is used by permission of Kids Can Press, illustration © Shelagh Armstrong 2002, John Lawrence/Stone; page 7 (top) Equator Graphics, Michael McQueen/Stone, Robert van der Hilst/Stone; page 8 Dennis Cox/China Stock; page 9 Jodi Cobb/NGS Image Collection; page 10 Yann Layma/Stone; page 11 Oriental Museum, Durham University, The Bridgeman Art Library; page 12 The Bridgeman Art Library; page 13 Phil Schmereister; page 16 (top) Kevin Supples, Keren Su/Stone; page 19 © Michael S. Yamashita/CORBIS; pages 22–23 (background) © MAPS.com/CORBIS, (top row left to right) Digital Vision/ Getty Images, Steven Curtis Design (pencil), PhotoDisc®, Steven Curtis Design, (bottom row left to right) Steven Curtis Design, © Hulton-Deutsch Collection/ CORBIS, Carl & Ann Purcell/CORBIS, Christopher Arnesen/ Stone; page 24 Icon art by John Haslam.

Info-Pal icon art by John Haslam.

Produced through the worldwide resources of the National Geographic Society, John M. Fahey, Jr., President and Chief Executive Officer; Gilbert M. Grosvenor, Chairman of the Board; Nina D. Hoffman, Executive Vice President and President, Books and Education Publishing Group.

Prepared by National Geographic School Publishing

Ericka Markman, Senior Vice President and President, Children's Books and Education Publishing Group; Steve Mico, Senior Vice President, Editorial Director; Marianne Hiland, Executive Editor; Jim Hiscott, Design Manager; Kristin Hanneman, Illustrations Manager; Matt Wascavage, Manager of Publishing Services; Sean Philpotts, Production Manager.

Manufacturing and Quality Control

Christopher A. Liedel, Chief Financial Officer; Phillip L. Schlosser, Director; Clifton M. Brown III, Manager

Program Consultants

Stephanie Harvey, National Educational Consultant, Colorado; Dr. P. David Pearson, Professor and Dean, University of California, Berkeley

Program Development

Mary Anne Wengel

Book Development

Morrison BookWorks

Book Design

Steven Curtis Design

Published by the National Geographic Society
1145 17th Street, N.W.
Washington, D.C. 20036–4688

ISBN: 0-7922-5048-6

Fourth Printing April 2005

Printed in Canada.

For more information on the comprehension strategies used in Nonfiction Reading and Writing Workshops, see *Strategies That Work: Teaching Comprehension to Enhance Understanding* by Stephanie Harvey and Anne Goudvis. ©2000. Stenhouse Publishers, www.stenhouse.com

Contents

Introduction

Comparing and Contrasting

Like these students, you may be asked to compare and contrast people, places, things, and events. When you **compare**, you look for ways things are alike. When you **contrast**, you look for ways things are different.

You may also be reading **nonfiction** that compares and contrasts. Here is what you need to know about compare-contrast writing.

All About Compare–Contrast Writing

- Compare-contrast writing shows how two or more people, places, things, or events are alike and different.

- The subjects being compared or contrasted are clearly stated.

- Both likenesses and differences are presented and explained.

- Special words called **clue words** help you know when things are being compared and contrasted.

In this book, you will learn the strategy of **asking questions** to help you understand comparisons as you read. Then you'll learn how to write your own compare-contrast essay.

More About Nonfiction

- Nonfiction writing provides **facts**—it's not made up. The facts can be proved.

- **Kinds of nonfiction** include your science and social studies books, biographies, autobiographies, letters, and informational books.

- Nonfiction has **features**, including subheads, photographs, captions, diagrams, maps, and words in **bold print.**

Many sources of information compare people, places, and things.

5

Part 1

Reading Workshop
Asking Questions

Understand the Strategy

Do you ask a lot of questions when you have a conversation with a friend? *What happened? Why did you do that? Did anything else happen?* We ask questions to make sure we understand what people mean. We listen to see if our questions are answered.

Asking questions when you read is like having a conversation with the author. Ask questions and look for the answers as you read. This will help you make sense of it all.

Strategy

Asking Questions

Ask lots of questions as you read. Ask them after you read too!

Asking Questions ⟶ Finding Answers

Asking Questions	Finding Answers
Ask questions about *how* you read. • Am I "getting" this? • I'm confused. What can I do?	**Reread** to see if you missed an important fact or a definition of a hard word. **Read on** to see if the confusion is cleared up.
Ask questions about *what* you read. • Why did that happen? • What does this word mean? • What will happen next? • What do I think about this?	**Read on** for answers to your questions. **Look for information** that helps you figure out the answer. **Remember** that some of your questions may not be answered in the article.
Ask questions to learn more. • What else do I want to know? • What do I wonder about?	**Share** your questions with others. **Think** about ways to find the answers.

Think As You Read

Use this routine as you read "Community Life" on pages 8–13. This article is from a book that compares and contrasts life in China long ago with life in China today.

1 **Preview the article.** Read the title and subheads. Look at the pictures. Ask yourself: *What will I be reading about?*

2 **Read the article one section at a time.**

3 **Think as you read.** Stop after you read each section. Ask yourself: *Am I "getting" this? What will I read about next?*

4 **Take notes as you read.** Write down questions you have. Write down any answers you find.

You can see two tools for taking notes below. Remember that some of your questions may not be answered!

5 **Share your ideas about what you read with a partner.**

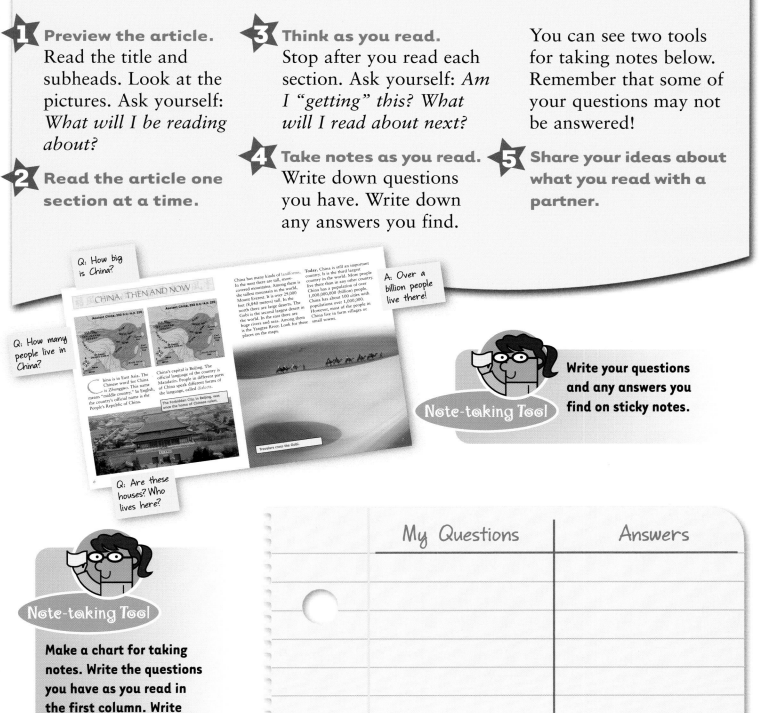

Q: How big is China?

Q: How many people live in China?

A: Over a billion people live there!

Q: Are these houses? Who lives here?

Note-taking Tool

Write your questions and any answers you find on sticky notes.

Note-taking Tool

Make a chart for taking notes. Write the questions you have as you read in the first column. Write answers you find in the second column.

My Questions	Answers

Practice and Apply the Strategy

Ask questions as you read about community life in China. Then read on to see if your questions are answered. The margin notes include questions one reader asked.

The title tells me the topic of the article.

The subhead tells me what this section is about.

The words "In ancient China" and "Today" are clue words. They point to a comparison or contrast coming up.

Q: Wooden pillows! How could they ever get to sleep?

福風亭 COMMUNITY LIFE 福風亭

HOUSES

In ancient China, three generations of a family often lived together in one house. There were rules about how family members acted. Children were taught to obey their parents. The grandparents, as the oldest, were the most respected.

Most people in ancient China were farmers. Farmers lived in simple one-story houses. The roofs were made of straw. Families slept on simple mats. They used wooden pillows. Houses had outdoor areas for cooking.

In China today, farmhouses have tile or straw roofs and are built of stone or clay bricks.

We know a lot more about the homes of the rich. The rich were sometimes buried with a clay model of their home. Their houses had two or more floors and tile roofs.

Today, Chinese farmers live in simple houses like those of long ago. Their houses are small and have few pieces of furniture. Toilets are outside. In the cities, most people live in crowded apartments. The apartments are built around courtyards. People living in an apartment building share the courtyard. Some apartments do not have baths. So, people use public baths in the cities.

LOOKING BACK

Did you know that the ancient Chinese did not use stone to build their houses? They used wood or bamboo, a tall, woody plant that grows in many places in China. The Chinese sometimes covered the walls with bricks or earth.

SCHOOL

Do you think you would like being a scholar? You would spend all your time studying and learning. Scholars were the most respected group in ancient times. Scholars could read and write. Most worked for the emperor, the ruler of the country.

These boys attend temple school.

LOOKING BACK

Working for the government was a good job. But very few could get this job. In later years, the odds of passing the palace test and getting a job were 3,000 to one!

In ancient China, only boys were educated. Sometimes a whole village would choose one young boy to become a scholar. This boy would then go on to the university. He would work for the emperor or in the government, called the Imperial Civil Service.

Girls learned to take care of the house. They also learned about silk. They learned how to raise silkworms which spun silk thread. The silk industry in China was developed and run by women.

Today, almost all children in China go to school. They start school at age six or seven. Children in the cities go to school for six full days each week. They have six weeks of vacation during the summer. They also have four weeks off in the winter. Children in the country take time off from school to work on the farms.

Q: In ancient China, girls didn't go to school. I wonder: Do girls go to school in China today?

A: Girls do go to school today. It says right here that almost all children go to school, so that includes girls.

What questions do you have as you read these two pages? Remember to write them down. Write down the answers you find too. One reader's questions are shown here.

This section is about farming.

Here are "In ancient China" and "Today" again. They point to a comparison or contrast coming up.

Q: What does a rice paddy look like?

A: So this is what a rice paddy looks like. But are the rice plants growing under all the water? Does the water just soak into the ground?

FARMING

In ancient China, many people lived in the country. They were farmers. They lived in small villages. Farmers were well respected in China. Farmers worked from dawn to dusk.

In northern China, farmers grew beans and grain, including wheat and barley. In the south, farmers grew rice in special fields called **paddies.** They flooded these fields with water from nearby rivers.

In early China, farmers used oxen to pull plows. They also used iron tools. They invented the wheelbarrow, which they called a "wooden ox." These improvements helped people farm better.

LOOKING BACK

Everyone in ancient China had to pay taxes. Farmers often paid their taxes with rice. They could also pay by working for the government, digging canals, or building walls. Farmers had to join the army for a period of time.

Today, farming is still important in China. More than half of the people in China are farmers or work on farms. China is the largest producer of food in the world. It has to feed over one billion people. Grain, such as rice and wheat, is China's most important crop. Large farms are run by the government. Much of the land is also owned by the government.

A water buffalo and farmers leave rice paddy fields in the evening.

Q: Will I be reading about the kind of Chinese food that we get in restaurants?

FOOD

In ancient China, poor families ate beans, other vegetables, and grains. They did not usually eat meat. Sometimes they ate chicken, fish, or wild birds. To save fuel, they chopped their food into small pieces. Then they cooked the pieces quickly in an iron frying pan, or wok. Families also steamed their food.

Rich families ate many different foods. Noodles, fruits, and vegetables were popular. Honey, cinnamon, peanuts, ginger, and salt added flavor to food. The rich also ate meat, including pork, deer, duck, and lamb. They even enjoyed eating snake, dog, and bear paws!

Tea was the most important drink. Some people became experts on tea. There were tea-tasting contests. Experts tried to tell which tea they were tasting.

Today, many Chinese eat some of the same foods that families ate long ago. Breakfast is often noodles, wheat bread, or rice porridge. The porridge is topped with shrimp, vegetables, or pickles.

The kitchen god

LOOKING BACK

The kitchen god was important in ancient China. The Chinese believed that the kitchen god reported how a family behaved during the year to the other gods. A bad report could mean bad luck for the next year. Families set off fireworks to honor the kitchen god.

The Chinese eat with chopsticks and soup spoons. They use knives only in the kitchen, not at the table. Silverware is thought to be in bad taste. Meals are either stir-fried in woks or steamed.

Q: Where do chopsticks come from?

A: We eat stir-fry, but not porridge. That sounds like something they eat in fairy tales.

Continue reading and asking questions. Be sure you write down your questions and any answers you find. Remember that some questions may not be answered. You may need to do further research to answer them.

CLOTHES

In ancient China, you could tell who was rich and who was poor by the clothes they wore. The poor wore clothes made from hemp. Hemp is a rough fabric woven from plant fibers. Clothes were loose with tunic-like tops and simple pants.

The rich wore robes made from silk. They also wore jewelry made of jade, gold, and silver. Sometimes men wore hats. A hat showed the wearer's job and social class.

Wealthy men in China used to wear fancy silk robes and hats.

LOOKING BACK

The colors of cloth were important to the ancient Chinese. Cloth was colored with vegetable dyes. Each color meant something special. Yellow was a royal color. Only the emperor could wear it. Other people dressed in blue or black. White was for mourning. Children could not wear white while their parents were still alive. Red was the color of luck.

The ancient Chinese thought that women should have very small feet. It was a sign of beauty. Girls had their feet bound so that their feet would not grow. This painful practice was stopped in 1902.

Today, many Chinese wear Western-style shirts and loosely fitting pants or dark suits that button at the neck. In the country, farmers wear clothes that are like those peasants wore long ago.

In cities, people tend to wear more modern clothes. Jeans, however, are very expensive. Some people have to save for a year to buy a pair of jeans. Few people wear silk.

Chinese men carry a paper dragon in a New Year's parade.

FESTIVALS AND GAMES

In ancient China, festivals and games were important. The most important festival was held at the New Year. This holiday lasted 15 days. Families got together. Relatives came from far away. People visited each other bringing gifts. It was considered bad luck to turn away visitors. The holiday ended with a parade that included dragons and lanterns. The Chinese believed that the dragon would bring good luck for the New Year.

Another important festival was Qingming. During this festival people honored their dead relatives. People brought food to the graves and "talked" to their relatives. They wished them good lives in the afterworld.

Children had little time for games. Most children worked on the farms. But during festivals they flew kites and played chess and Chinese checkers. They also had a toy that is like our modern yo-yo.

Today, the Chinese New Year is still a popular holiday. Chinese around the world celebrate it. Chinese New Year starts no earlier than January 20 and no later than February 20. There are fireworks and parades with huge paper dragons. Children receive red envelopes with money and sometimes oranges for good luck.

Check Understanding

You've now read a great deal about how people lived in China! Check your notes to see if they help you answer these questions.

- *What parts of community life does the author compare and contrast?*

- *How is community life in ancient China like community life in modern China? How is it different?*

Now fill in a diagram like the one below to show your thinking. On the left, write details that apply only to ancient China. On the right, write details that apply only to modern China. In the middle, write details that apply to both ancient and modern China. Look at the sample before you begin.

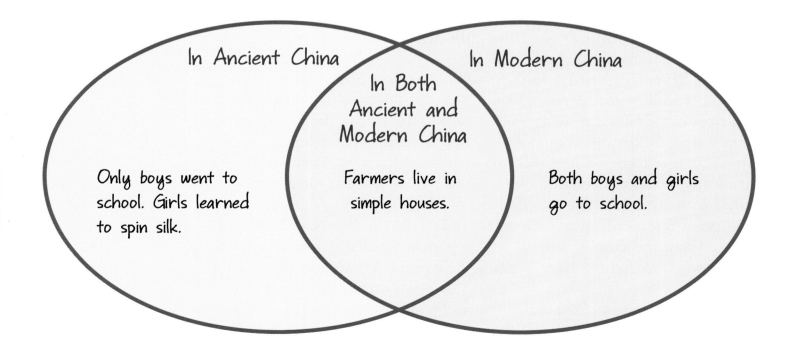

In Ancient China

In Both Ancient and Modern China

In Modern China

Only boys went to school. Girls learned to spin silk.

Farmers live in simple houses.

Both boys and girls go to school.

Share and Respond

Can you think of a song that makes you smile, but makes your friend change the station? Two people who read the same article don't always have the same response to it either. Think about your response to "Community Life." Then talk with a partner. Ask each other:

- *What information did you find surprising?*
- *What information was new and interesting?*
- *What do you still wonder about?*

Write a Response

Choose a subject such as houses, clothing, school, food, farming, or festivals and write a response to it. In your response,

- Include information from the article
- Relate the article to something else
- Tell what you still wonder about

Here's one reader's response.

We read "Community Life." This was about ways people in China lived long ago and how they live today. I liked the part about only boys going to school. In ancient China, girls didn't go to school. Only boys went. And sometimes, only one boy in a whole village went to college. Girls stayed home. But they got to learn all about silkworms and how they spin silk. I read a book about this once and it showed beautiful pictures of the cocoons the silk worms spin. I guess it would be more fun than going to school, but I still wonder how you could work with the worms on a farm and have your feet all bound up. My teacher said that was very painful. How could you walk to work? I still wonder about that.

The writer included information from the article.

The writer related the article to something else.

The writer included what he wonders.

Writing Workshop
Compare-Contrast Essay

Author's Chair

An Interview with Kevin Supples

Kevin Supples has written several books about life in other countries. "Community Life" is from his book called *China*. We interviewed Mr. Supples about his writing.

Q Why did you choose to write about China?

A *China is a huge, fascinating country. One out of every four people on Earth lives there. China is also one of the oldest civilizations in the world.*

Q How do you find your information?

A *I read a lot of books! I try to find recent titles, and I also look for information in magazines and newspapers.*

Q Why did you decide to compare ancient and modern China?

A *I think readers enjoy finding out how places and customs change and yet stay the same.*

Q What's the most important thing you want readers to learn from your book about China?

A *That's a difficult question. I hope they will learn that there are many similarities and connections between people from different cultures. That's important to me.*

Writers usually write best about subjects that interest them. Over the next few pages, you will learn how to write an essay that **compares and contrasts** two subjects you are interested in. You might want to write about life in your own community.

Prewriting

Focus on Content and Organization

Choose Subjects to Compare

Begin by listing things you could compare. Think of things that share both likenesses and differences. You might think about subjects that have something to do with your town or school.

Fourth of July and Thanksgiving   Buying your lunch and bringing it
Swimming and ice-skating   from home
                                                         Cole School ten years ago and today

List Details About Each Subject

After you decide on your subjects, think about them. Start listing details that tell about each subject. This will help you identify details to compare.

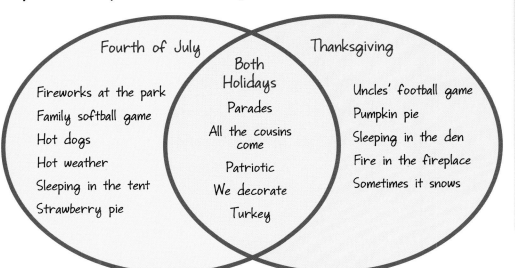

Fourth of July
Fireworks at the park
Family softball game
Hot dogs
Hot weather
Sleeping in the tent
Strawberry pie

Both Holidays
Parades
All the cousins come
Patriotic
We decorate
Turkey

Thanksgiving
Uncles' football game
Pumpkin pie
Sleeping in the den
Fire in the fireplace
Sometimes it snows

Reading/Writing Connection

Your **compare-contrast essay** should

- Introduce the subjects you will compare

- Explain both the likenesses and differences

- Use **clue words** that make comparisons and contrasts clear, for example, *both, neither, only*

Audience and Purpose

Before you write, remember what the purpose of your essay is and who you want to read it. For example:

Purpose: Compare and contrast my favorite holidays

Audience: Students my age

Organize and Plan Your Writing

Here are two ways to organize your essay. Choose the way that fits how you want to write.

Organize by Subjects Organize your essay around your **subjects,** for example, *Fourth of July* and *Thanksgiving.* With this plan, most of your comparing and contrasting will be in Part 2.

Organize by Details You can also organize your essay around the **details,** for example, *food* and *fun things to do.* In this plan, you compare and contrast in each part.

Organizing by Subjects

Part 1 4th of July

    Describe the foods we eat and the fun things we do on the Fourth of July

Part 2 Thanksgiving

    Compare and contrast the foods we eat and the fun we have on the Fourth of July with the foods we eat and the fun things we do on Thanksgiving

Organizing by Details

Part 1 Food

    Compare and contrast the foods we eat on the Fourth of July with the foods we eat on Thanksgiving

Part 2 Fun Things to Do

    Compare and contrast the fun things we do on the Fourth of July with the fun things we do on Thanksgiving

Write Your First Two Sentences

People who travel to new places need maps. People who read need maps too. In a compare-contrast essay, the reader needs to know early on where he or she is going—that is, what the author will compare. Write your first two sentences. This will help you focus your writing.

Two of my favorite holidays are the Fourth of July and Thanksgiving. Each holiday has great food and fun things to do.

— Subjects

— Details

Drafting

Focus on Voice

It's time to start writing. Don't worry about getting everything right the first time. Just write! You'll have a chance to go back and fix things you don't like. Remember to try to sound like yourself as you write. Here's what one reader wrote.

Writing Tip

Use the article on pages 8-13 as a model. What clue words can you use to help your reader?

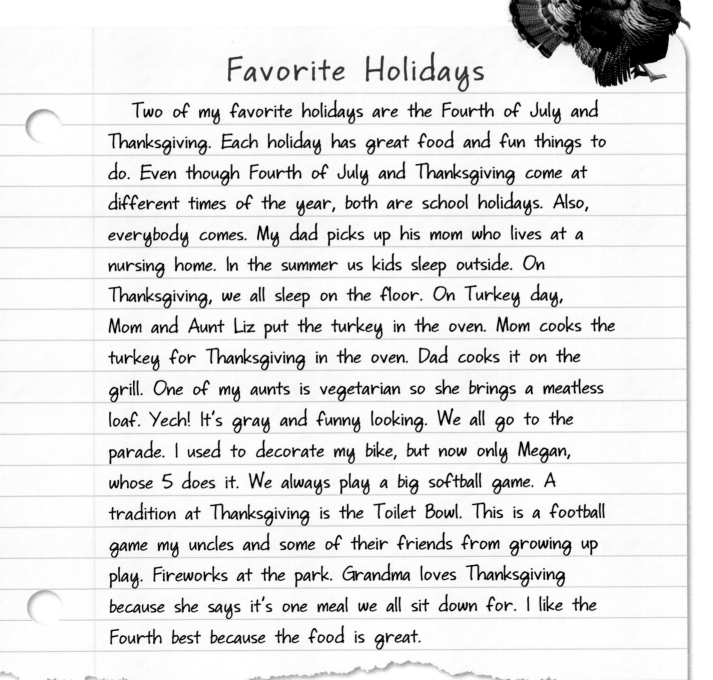

Favorite Holidays

Two of my favorite holidays are the Fourth of July and Thanksgiving. Each holiday has great food and fun things to do. Even though Fourth of July and Thanksgiving come at different times of the year, both are school holidays. Also, everybody comes. My dad picks up his mom who lives at a nursing home. In the summer us kids sleep outside. On Thanksgiving, we all sleep on the floor. On Turkey day, Mom and Aunt Liz put the turkey in the oven. Mom cooks the turkey for Thanksgiving in the oven. Dad cooks it on the grill. One of my aunts is vegetarian so she brings a meatless loaf. Yech! It's gray and funny looking. We all go to the parade. I used to decorate my bike, but now only Megan, whose 5 does it. We always play a big softball game. A tradition at Thanksgiving is the Toilet Bowl. This is a football game my uncles and some of their friends from growing up play. Fireworks at the park. Grandma loves Thanksgiving because she says it's one meal we all sit down for. I like the Fourth best because the food is great.

Revising and Editing

Focus on Word Choice

After you have written down your ideas, it's time to sit back and read your draft. As you read, ask yourself:

- *Do I need to add or take out information?*
- *Do I need to rearrange anything?*
- *Will this be interesting to kids my age?*

Favorite Holidays

Two of my favorite holidays are the Fourth of July and Thanksgiving. Each holiday has great food and fun things to do. Even though Fourth of July and Thanksgiving come at different times of the year, both are school holidays. Also, ~~everybody~~ *all our cousins* comes. My dad picks up his mom who lives at a nursing home. ~~In the summer us kids sleep outside. On Thanksgiving, we all sleep on the floor.~~ On Turkey day, Mom and Aunt Liz put the turkey in the oven. ~~Mom cooks the turkey for Thanksgiving in the oven.~~ *On the Fourth, outside* Dad cooks it on the grill. ~~One of my aunts is vegetarian so she brings a meatless~~

¶ We have great food on both days⊙ We always have turkey⊙

¶ We have lots of fun on each holiday⊙

Revising Checklist

- Do I introduce the subjects I will compare?
- Do I explain how each subject is like and different from the other?
- Is my essay organized by subjects or by details?
- Do I need more information?
- Have I written a conclusion or did I just stop writing?

Zoom in for Details

Do you need to add information to your essay? Imagine you are looking at your writing with a powerful lens. Now zoom in. If you can't clearly "see" what you've written about, you need to add information.

Original
On Turkey Day, Mom and Aunt Liz put the turkey in the oven.

Revised
Mom and Aunt Liz are up at dawn putting the turkey in the oven. They're so noisy! They laugh and sing oldies—loud and off-key.

Edit

Take the time to read over your final essay. Check your spelling and punctuation. Read each sentence to make sure it is clear and interesting. Do you begin and end each sentence correctly?

Proofreading Marks

Take out	⤴	Capital letter	≡
Insert	∧	Spelling	◯
Small letter	/	New paragraph	¶

Sharing and Publishing

Make a Book

Did several of you write about your community? If so, you might put the essays together in a book for students new to your community. Think about what the cover, title page, and contents page should look like.

Author's Chair

Interview individual authors in your class. Ask them how they planned and carried out their essays. Authors can read a portion to help explain their ideas.

School Website

Work with a partner to create a home page for your essay. Use photos from magazines or create illustrations and artwork to help explain your ideas. If possible, post your home page on the school website.

Extend
On Assignment

Look Back

In this book you used the strategy for asking questions. You also learned how to plan and write a compare-contrast essay. What would you tell the students on page 4 about reading and writing comparisons?

Learn More

You can use what you have learned about reading and writing to learn more about community life—in China or in your own community. Go "On Assignment" with one or more of the following activities.

Assignment 1

Map the Continents

China is in East Asia, on the continent of Asia. What's a continent? How many continents are there? Where in the world are they?

Your assignment: Use an atlas to learn about continents. Then create a poster or set of maps for someone your age. Show where the continents are in the world. Label the continents and the big bodies of water that surround the continents.

China

Assignment 2

Your Town: Then and Now

"Community Life" is from a book called *China*. In it, the author describes ways ancient and modern China are alike and different. What would a similar book about your town be like?

Your assignment: Write an essay that compares a feature of your town fifty or one hundred years ago with today. Find books or photographs of your town at the library. Ask an older person how life in your town has changed. Gather your facts and then write your essay.

Assignment 3

The China Game

The tallest mountain. The oldest civilization. The highest population. Yes, China is a land of extremes. What other questions did you have as you read?

Your assignment: Create your own China Pursuit game for you and your friends and family. Use an almanac, an atlas, and other references to get facts about China. Turn the facts into a question-and-answer game. (Don't make it too hard.) Decide how your game should be played. Then invite your friends and family to test their China knowledge.

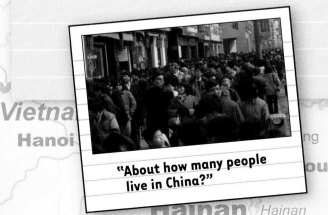

"About how many people live in China?"

Assignment 4

Sketch the Great Wall

The Great Wall of China may be the most famous wall in the world! Where is it? What does it look like? What makes it so great?

Your assignment: Research the Great Wall of China. Then sketch a section of it. Label your sketch to show the dimensions, materials, and other interesting facts you want to show.

Sources You Can Use

Check out these Internet sites and books when you go "On Assignment."

Discovering China
Learn about the history, people, and culture of China.
http://library.thinkquest.org/26469/

Henry Ford Museum and Greenfield Village
Visit the museum to see the "Your Place in Time" exhibit and visit the village to experience farm life in the late 1800s, railroads, and the development of American culture.
http://www.hfmgv.org/

Made in China—Explorations
Explore the science, culture, and industry of the world's oldest civilization. Experience the foods, architecture, history, and transportation in the great cities of Hong Kong, Shanghai, Beijing, and Nanjing.
http://china.candidemedia.com/html/index.html

Secrets of the Great Wall
Discover how the Great Wall was built by the Qin, Han, and Ming dynasties.
http://www.discovery.com/stories/history/greatwall/greatwall.html

Ancient China
by Arthur Cotterell
Discover the history of China through life, crafts, culture, and architecture.
Alfred A. Knopf, 1994.

House
by Albert Lorenz
From Ancient Egypt to outer space, the houses in this book show how people live throughout the world.
Harry N. Abrams, Inc. 1998.

My Backyard History Book
by David Weitzman
This is a great guide to researching your genealogy and your town's history.
Little, Brown and Company, 1975.

River Town and Prairie Town
by Bonnie and Arthur Geisert
These two books explore the origins and daily life of towns that grew up near rivers and railroads over 100 years ago.
Houghton Mifflin Company, 1999.

World Atlas for Young Explorers
by National Geographic Society
This reference shows world, regional, and thematic maps and photo essays about the continents.
National Geographic Society, 1998.